IMAGES
*of America*

# THE 1964 FLOOD OF HUMBOLDT AND DEL NORTE

ON THE COVER: Hanging on perilously, this storefront was no match for the surging floodwaters of the Eel River. The river destroyed numerous bridges and roadways and cut off the towns along the river from aid for days. This store eventually lost its fight with gravity and plunged into the raging river below.

IMAGES
*of America*

# THE 1964 FLOOD OF HUMBOLDT AND DEL NORTE

Greg Rumney and Dave Stockton Jr.

ARCADIA
PUBLISHING

Published by Arcadia Publishing
Charleston, South Carolina

Library of Congress Control Number: 2013910001

For all general information, please contact Arcadia Publishing:
Telephone 843-853-2070
Fax 843-853-0044
E-mail sales@arcadiapublishing.com
For customer service and orders:
Toll-Free 1-888-313-2665

Visit us on the Internet at www.arcadiapublishing.com

*To my wife, Penny*

# CONTENTS

# ACKNOWLEDGMENTS

This book would not have been possible without the stories and pictures of those who experienced this flood firsthand. Rudy Gillard started his photographic career in the late 1940s after he and his wife, Jenny, moved to Fortuna from the Oakland area. He set up shop, doing portraits and other work, on Main Street in Fortuna. In 1964, Rudy became the official photographer to document the devastating and unprecedented Christmas flood of 1964. When Rudy was about to retire, he donated all his negatives to Greg Rumney to insure the preservation of the past would be carried on. This donation included several thousand negatives and images of the Christmas flood of 1964. This book presents a small sample of some of his best images. Rudy passed away in 2009.

We would also like to thank Ray Evans, the late Robert Childs, Charley and Betty Thomas, and David Carneggie for not only sharing photographs but also firsthand experiences of the flood and its aftermath. We are also indebted to Susan O'Hara for some duplicates from the *Humboldt Redwoods State Park* book. The full story of the flood could not be told without these important photographs. Humboldt Redwoods Interpretive Association has helped with information and excerpts from *The Killer Eel*, a 32-page magazine published in 1965. The Fortuna Depot Museum has also assisted with the text. A special thanks goes to Penny Rumney for all her hard work from the beginning, scanning and organizing the overall project. A story of this size and impact cannot be completely told from these pictures, but those that have been contributed will give the reader a good feel of the event. All images appear courtesy of Rudy Gillard.

# INTRODUCTION

The 1964 flood was one of those perfect storms. All the weather events lined up in a sequence that maximized the runoff of rivers and streams over five states. Northern California and Southern Oregon were the hardest hit and were directly in the path of the brunt of the storms. There were three main components to this perfect storm, and these three focused on the 3,684-square-mile drainage of the Eel River and its tributaries along with the 15,751-square-mile Klamath River drainage. The first part of the storm began around December 13, 1964, with a cold front from the north moving in and dropping a few feet of snow. After this storm was spent, a warm storm from the south, locally called the "pineapple connection," moved in and dropped 22 to 37 inches of rain in three days and over 30 for the week. The volume was so intense that drivers who turned their windshield wipers on high speed still could not keep the water off long enough to see. As if this were not enough, the third component of this perfect storm was the highest tide of the year that came during the peak hours of the flood crest. This caused a damming effect on some of the bridges that raised water levels to record highs. Locals believed that the Eel River would drop for at least eight hours—no matter the weather conditions— as soon as it crested; however, this time, the Eel River stayed at a near maximum for almost 24 hours, an unheard-of event on the Eel River drainage.

Residents along the Eel River were no strangers to high waters and floods. A tried-and-true method employed by the old-timers to check water levels was to drive a stake at the water's edge and come back in a half hour. This would enable the resident to calculate the water's increase per hour and, coupled with the weather forecast or a reported crest from the south drainage, a rough estimate of how high the river would rise. At the time of the flood, there was also the mind-set that the Eel and Klamath Rivers could get no higher because many experts had said that the 1955 flood was the "1,000-year flood." The locals soon realized that the rate of rise was double that of 1955, and from there, with the rain as intense as it was, there was no telling how high both rivers could go. Ferndale and Fernbridge were both hit hard. Fernbridge, with it businesses, such as the Challenge Creamery and Barnes Tractor, all next to the main Eel River, and Ferndale, with its dairy herds and barns, were victims not only to the water, but also piles of logs from the lumber operations upstream. Both were so close to the mouth of the river that drift was caught almost anyplace with a natural barrier. One happy story that came out of Ferndale was that a cow with her herd number tag came into the harbor at Crescent City, about 85 miles north, three days after the peak of the flood. The cow was fine but very hungry. In a few weeks, she was returned to her herd in Ferndale. There were several veterans of the 1937 flood and a few from the 1915 flood, and all were unanimous that 1964 flood was far worse than any deluge they had seen. Both the 1915 and 1937 floods left remnants behind to build on, and residents took it in stride. The 1955 flood saw the loss of two communities, Dyerville and Elinor. These losses were of great consequence and were as much of a moral blow as a physical one. These destructive floods, however, would pale in comparison to the great Christmas flood of 1964.

In anticipation of floodwaters, the towns along the Eel River, such as Loleta, Ferndale, Fernbridge, Lower Fortuna, Alton, Metropolitan, Rio Dell, Scotia, Pepperwood, Shively, Holmes, Larabee,

South Fork, Weott, Myers Flat, Phillipsville, and Sylvandale, started evacuating days before the initial storm. Businesses moved their inventories to high ground as some private homes were also emptied of what could be carried. In many cases, people living where the rivers had never been before took what they could and moved to higher ground. Most, when their items were safe, returned to help neighbors. Those with the mind-set that the flood of 1955 was the worst possible hung on until it was obvious this flood was beyond what anyone had seen. A strange phenomenon reported by residents was a deep, unsettling roar when the river was extremely high; the sound was similar to that of a strong earthquake—a haunting sound of out-of-control violence.

Food and shelter were immediate issues following the flood. People with freezers or any food storage device opened them up to the community to feed all that were hungry. Residents whose homes survived the flood provided shelter until disaster relief came. Many remarked it was a shame it took a disaster of this scale to bring people together to share all they had. There was a great sense of community for several months following.

People along the rivers had experienced disasters before and prepared town centers for food and other necessities to be shared. Security and communication systems were set up to the outside world to restore as much semblance of normalcy as possible. Along both rivers, what could be saved or salvaged was done as much as possible. Many people recognized possessions downstream that belonged to their neighbors, and these items were returned.

When the water did go down, resident were in shocked disbelief when they returned to their homes and businesses. It was as if it were a deeply personal violation, like a robbery, that forcibly and violently took something of their essence. Many structures were completely gone. There were whole sections of Ferndale, Metropolitan, Stafford, Pepperwood, Shively, Holmes, Larabee, South Fork, Weott, Myers Flat, Phillipsville, and Sylvandale that were wiped clean. Structures that remained were in states of major to total damage. Those who lost everything could breathe a sigh of relief and begin again clean. Many who had been through the 1955 flood gave up after losing everything twice. Others who still had some possessions remaining had the disheartening task of trying to save what they could, only to find there was little to save—all that work for so little to be recovered.

There were different estimates of the volume of water coming down the Eel River. In Scotia, one estimate was 752,000 cubic feet of water per second on the morning of December 23. Some estimates were made in acre-feet per second. Agencies involved did agree that the volume of water at the mouth of the Eel River would be at flood stage for the Columbia River and flood stage for the Mississippi River. Sediment loads for the Eel River were estimated at a million cubic yards per day. There were no estimates for the amount of debris that came down the river, but the beaches in Humboldt and Del Norte Counties were littered for miles. There were reports that, by the summer of 1965, a lot of flood debris washed up on some of the islands of Japan.

The Van Duzen River is a 63-mile-long tributary that empties into the main Eel River about 10 miles east of the mouth. Damage along the Van Duzen River in the low areas included the loss of a major bridge on Highway 36 along with many homes. In Bridgeville, some 25 miles from the mouth of the river, 48,000 cubic feet per second was estimated at the peak of the flooding.

The Klamath River is the second-largest river in California. Beginning in Klamath Falls, Oregon, the river travels 263 miles across California and empties into the Pacific Ocean near the town of Klamath, California. The river travels through five mountain ranges, beginning with the Southern Cascades, then into the western Klamath Mountains, then the Siskiyou Mountains, past the Trinity Mountains, and ending in the Coast Range. Tributaries begin with the Shasta River, then the Scott River, the Salmon River, and lastly, the Trinity River. The average flow in the dry months is 17,010 cubic feet per second as compared to the Eel River at Scotia's average flow of 7,315 cubic feet per second. At the peak of the flood, it was estimated that flows from 557,000 to 583,000 cubic feet per second were recorded. This is about 200,000 cubic feet per second lower than the Eel River at Scotia. In the town of Klamath, the water was about 15 feet deep on the highway and business district. The new Douglass Memorial Bridge was partially washed away; its washout was eerily similar to that of the old Douglass Memorial Bridge in the 1955 flood.

This view, looking east up the Klamath River, shows what remains of the town of Klamath. Prior to 1964, the town was also destroyed in the 1955 flood, in which the Golden Bear Bridge was partially damaged.

Work crews are shown using a pile driver on the Douglas Memorial Bridge, which was also known as the Golden Bear Bridge. Crews worked around the clock to finish the construction of the bridge, as it was a major artery to the north. Without this bridge, commerce came to a slow crawl as there is no other way to travel on Highway 101.

# *One*

# DEL NORTE COUNTY

In this view looking over the town of Klamath, one can see the destruction caused by the raging waters of the Klamath River. At its peak, the river was flowing over 500,000 cubic feet per minute, carrying rocks and giant redwood trees that acted like missiles and destroying everything in its path.

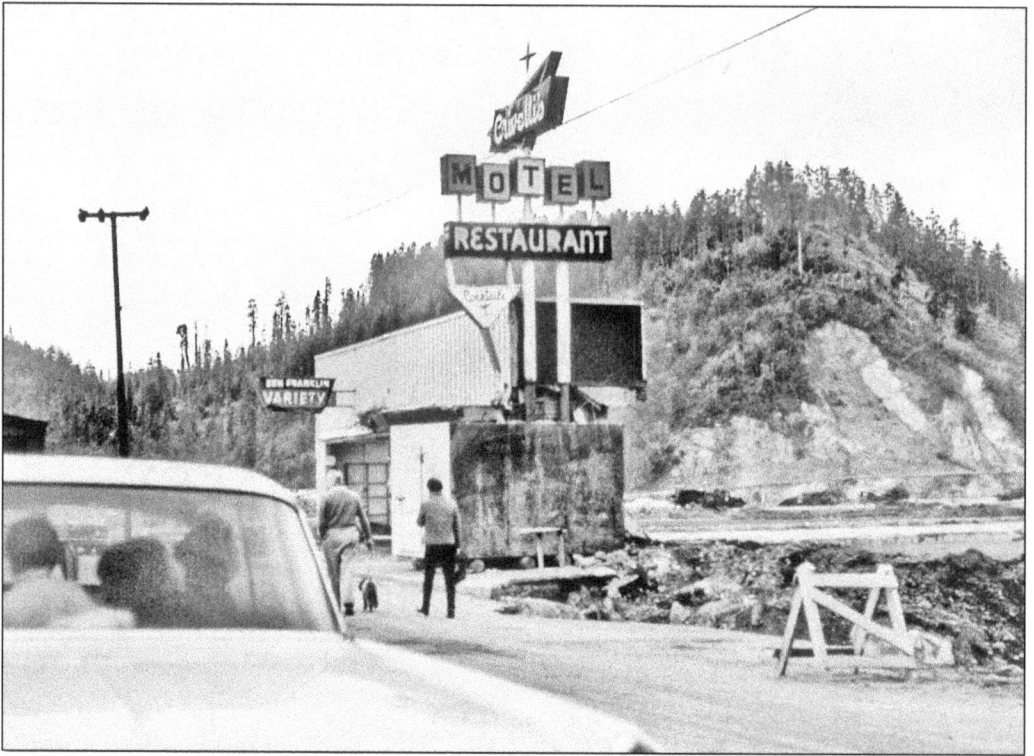

Locals walk past what is left of the Crivellis's Motel and Restaurant and the Ben Franklin Variety Store. The flood was not kind to this small Northern California town. Many people moved for good after suffering two major floods, both within 10 years of each other.

Armed men stand outside of the Klamath Liquor Store and the Steelhead Cafe, protecting what had become the most valuable commodities in town—liquor and food. Looting was a problem all along the flood-ravaged area of the north coast, as people were cut off from all sources of food and fuel for quite some time.

Jack West's Tavern and Cafe and the Klamath Sports Center Cafe are blocked by the mounds of wooden debris left by the raging Klamath River. Most locals thought that the river would never rise any higher than it did in 1955 when, in fact, it rose over five feet higher.

This scene shows the segment of the Douglas Memorial Bridge that was washed away by the floodwaters. Not many bridges were spared during this flood, as old-growth redwood trees weighing 20 tons or more smashed into these spans with horrific force.

Boats are seen pushing a barge carrying people to the other side of the Klamath River. Up until the river receded and barges and boats were brought in, the people of Klamath were stranded. For many residents, there were little to no resources.

This shot shows a road being reopened to begin repairs on the Douglas Memorial Bridge. Note the golden bears at the entrance of the bridge. The two bears weigh in at eight tons together. A new bridge has been built, but one can still view the old bridge with its original golden bears just downstream.

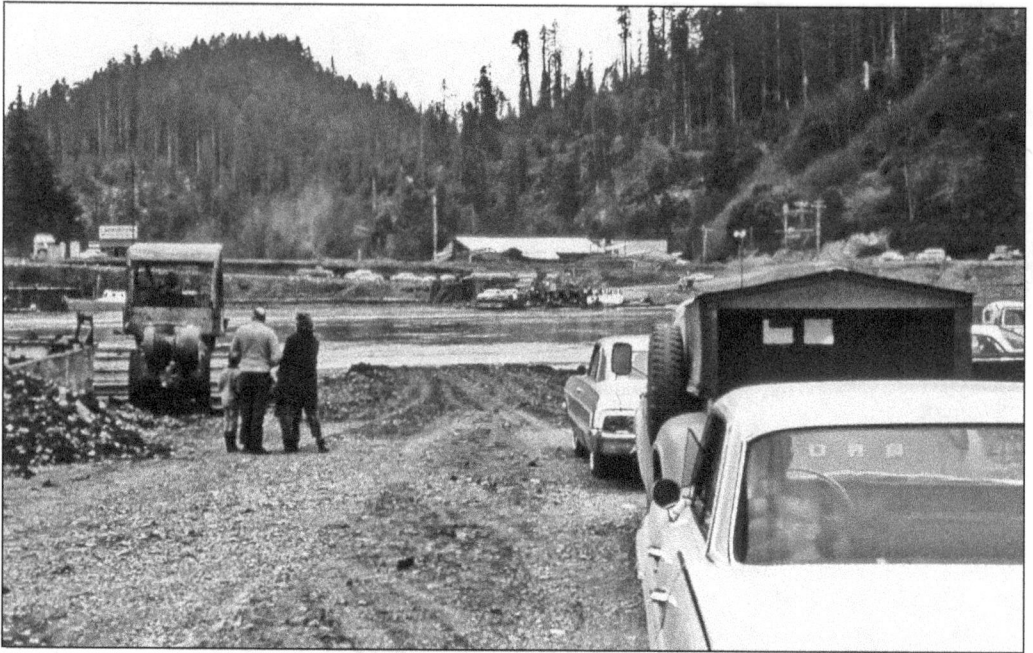

Local residence wait their turn at the river's edge to load onto the ferry to cross the Klamath River. People do not realize how much work went into installing a ferry system when all the roads into and out of this area were all but destroyed. Without the help of individual boat owners, many people would have been completely shut off, with no access to food and other supplies.

This aerial view shows Patrick's Creek Lodge and what was left of Highway 199, which was nearly destroyed by the Smith River. This famous lodge is still in operation today along the beautiful Smith River corridor, which goes to Grants Pass, Oregon.

Highway 199 looks calm in this
scene of the bridge missing over
the Smith River. This flood
took out so many bridges. The
Smith River at Dr. Fine Bridge on
December 22, 1964, was at 39.5 feet.
Thankfully, there were not many
towns along this stretch of river.

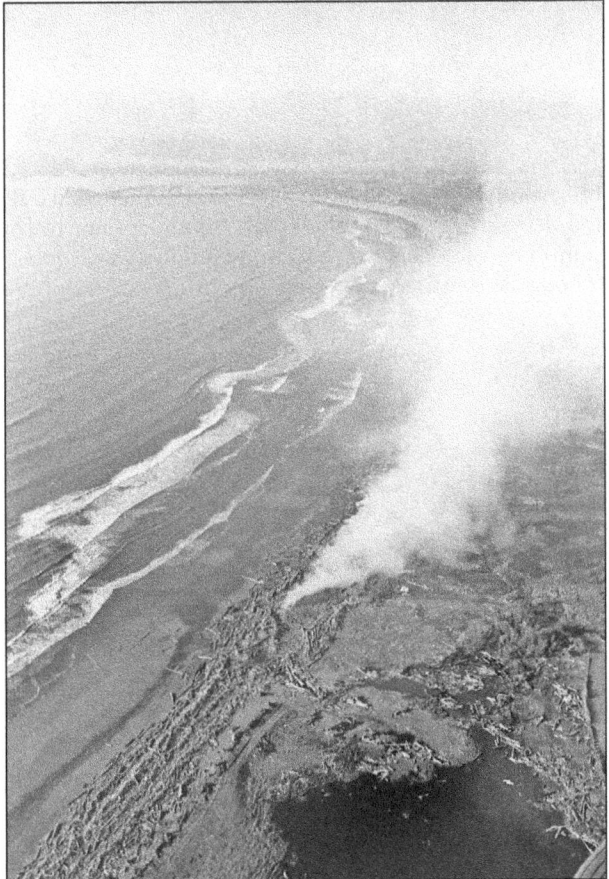

In this aerial view of Crescent City,
a fire is seen as people try to burn
off the remnants left from the log
decks that floated from the various
rivers. It was reported that there was
over 300 lumber mills in Humboldt
and Del Norte Counties, and
many lost their whole inventories
of logs and lumber, which created
these massive piles of wood.

This southeast scene of the beach at Crescent City shows the tremendous amounts of wood and debris that clogged the beach from Crescent to the Mattole River and beyond. Hundreds of millions of dollars worth of wood products were lost to the raging waters of the six rivers that encompass these two counties.

# Two

# FERNBRIDGE AND FERNDALE

This amazing image was taken looking north toward Fernbridge; one can see various ranches underwater and State Route 211 barely visible.

This photograph shows what was left of the fertile land around Ferndale. These areas are known for their prize dairy cows, most of which were lost in the flood.

This photograph was taken from atop Fernbridge, looking west, when the river was above flood stage. The buildings on the right are part of the Humboldt Creamery.

This photograph was taken of the Ferndale bottoms and shows the mouth of the Eel River on the left.

This photograph shows the extent of the raging Eel River as it swallows up Port Kenyon. There is water as far as the eye can see.

This was a typical scene along the Ferndale bottoms as most Victorian-era houses were destroyed by the Eel River. What was once a beautiful home and lush yard was reduced to rubble and gravel.

Here is another scene of the Ferndale bottoms. Most ranchers were caught off guard as the rivers had never risen to these levels before. Numerous families had to be rescued by boats and helicopters. And the animals were left to fend for themselves.

This view in this photograph, looking toward Loleta, shows the extent of how high the Eel River actually rose. The entire valley between Loleta and Ferndale was completely underwater.

Roads were turned into rivers, as seen in this photograph of Ferndale. Unfortunately, there were only two ways to escape, and one was closed. Only the Wildcat Road to Petrolia was open.

Help was on the way, as seen here. It came in the form of a Coast Guard helicopter, which was out on a search-and-rescue mission along the Ferndale bottoms. Unfortunately, there were two separate helicopter crashes that took the lives of four people in one and seven in the other.

There were so many scenes like this along the Ferndale and Loleta bottoms. Small homesites were totally encircled by water with no way to get out.

Looking toward Barnes Tractor in Fernbridge, one sees the amount of debris that came down the river. Fernbridge Bridge, also known as the "Queen of Bridges," was one of the only span to survive the brutal pounding of the giant redwood logs slamming into it.

In this view looking west toward Fernbridge, the water has almost reached the top of the bridge in the distance. The Queen of Bridges stood strong and survived the worst flood in history.

This aerial view shows the extent of the raging Eel River. Floodwaters stretched across the valley from the small town of Fernbridge to the Victorian village of Ferndale.

26

This scene was all too familiar as civilians and Coast Guard personnel rescued people from rooftops and small boats. This young girl, most likely a member of the Vineyard family, was rescued from the Loleta bottoms.

This view looking down Highway 211 toward Ferndale shows the width of the Eel River. There is a logjam beginning to build up along Fernbridge, but thankfully, a crane was brought in to remove the logs and debris. The Humboldt Creamery building is seen on the right, and Barnes Tractor is on the left of the bridge.

Here is Ferndale with Grizzly Bluff in the foreground; this photograph was taken when the river was beyond flood stage. Flowing into the Eel River near here, the raging Van Duzen River only made matters worse.

As the water receded, scenes like this were very common along the Ferndale and Loleta bottoms, with empty ranch houses and not an animal in sight. Though the ranchers tried to save their cows, many panicked and swam back into the torrential waters after being led back to dry ground.

This incredible photograph shows a ranch building missing part of its roof due to floodwaters. There are some cows on the right; normally, one would see a field full of dairy cows.

When the river finally went down, residents along the path of the Eel River returned to this muddy scene. Note slanted power lines and the mountains of debris.

This is the southern Fernbridge approach at peak flood stage. The Stevens home, pictured, withstood the raging river but was knocked off its foundation. Today, this site is a large parking lot used to unload various off-road vehicles.

This brave crane operator is desperately trying to remove the logjam before it gets too large and takes out the Queen of Bridges.

This soon-to-be logjam is behind the John Deere dealership. Logs from four or five lumber mills wreaked havoc on the bridges along the Eel and Van Duzen Rivers. A crane was brought in to try to save the famous bridge.

As the river receded, reality set in, and people wondered when and how the area was going to be cleaned up. Pictured is Route 211 from Fernbridge to Ferndale.

The back of the John Deere dealership looks like a bomb went off. Located on the riverbank of the Eel, the dealership suffered major losses. As seen in this photograph, large trees and water did not mix well with buildings.

Taken looking west toward the Pacific Ocean, with Ferndale in the far distance, this photograph depicts how flat the area really is because water takes the path of least resistance. The mouth of the Eel could not handle the volume of water being generated by the Eel and Van Duzen Rivers.

Here, water pours into Humboldt Creamery; the flood almost destroyed this world-famous dairy industry. Dairymen were forced to drain their milk onto the ground because they could not get the milk delivered to the creamery.

Pictured is a semisubmerged wind-powered water pump. The area usually is a beautiful pasture of green grass, and the very fertile silt from the Eel River actually helped the pastures years later.

Here, a boat returns flood victims to dry ground in the Ferndale bottoms. Civilians jumped in and helped the Coast Guard rescue family and friends, and they sometimes had to be rescued themselves if the motors on their boats were damaged by submerged obstacles in the water.

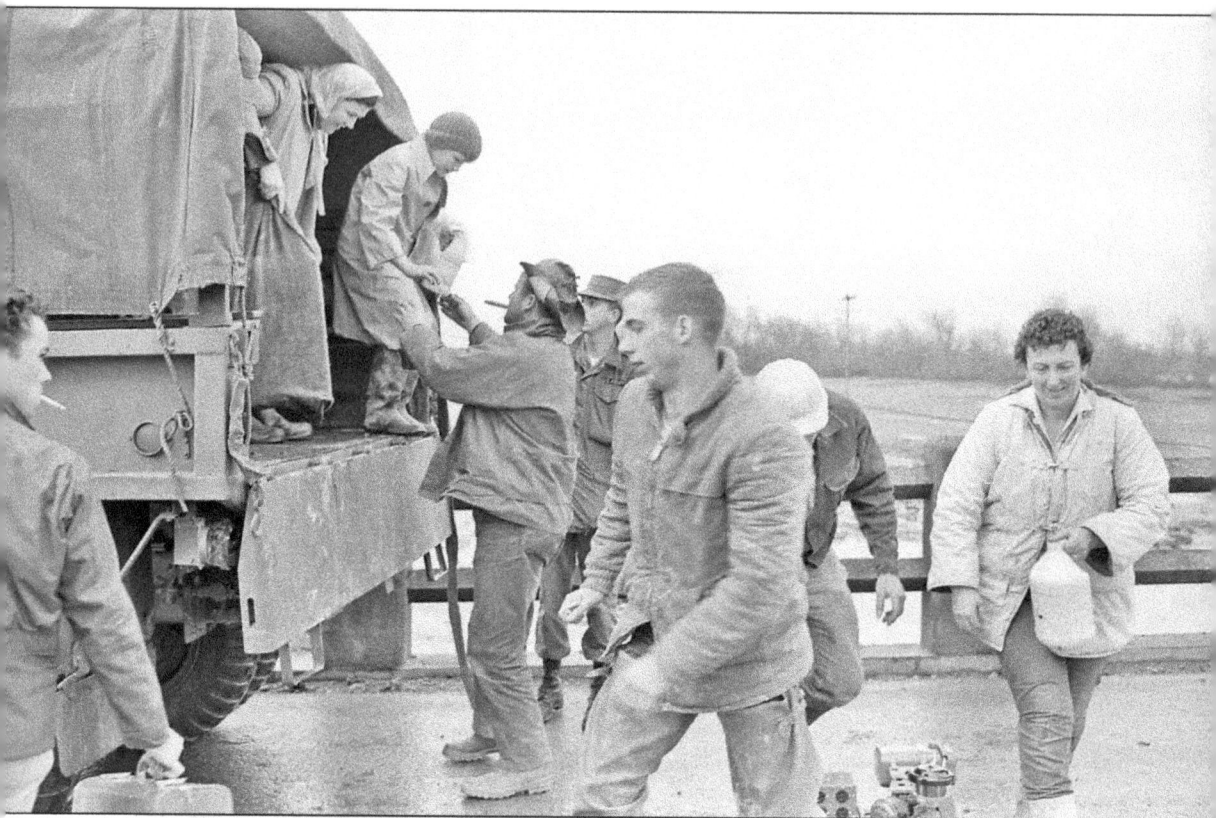

Army personnel helped unload people from a truck; the civilians were evacuated from the outlying areas around Ferndale.

*Three*

# FORTUNA

When this dike started bubbling, it was the first sign that something was not right with the embankment along Fortuna's Twelfth Street. It was the weak link in the 10-year-old gravel dike system.

This ruptured section of the dike was the result of the bubbling. As the dike broke, water roared into the lush fields of Fortuna and made its way into Kenmar Road area, carrying logs and other debris.

As the result of the break in the dike, this lumber mill was inundated in minutes.

This aerial view of the mill shows how the water was swirling in a vortex, making these large logs huge projectiles. The logs destroyed anything in their path, including the teepee burner.

Several lumber mills were operating on Twelfth Street at the time of the flood.

This aerial view, looking west at the break in the levee, shows how widespread the damage is. The Clay-Brown Mill is seen underwater. Right where the break is seen is where the current River Lodge Conference Center sits.

This photograph was taken from the area of present-day Royal Crest Mobile Estates. One can see an outline of the levee and floodwaters from Kenmar Road to the town of Alton to the south. Today's local gun club is found where the two small buildings are located.

The levees built in the 1950s were no match for the raging Eel and Van Duzen Rivers; almost all were breached.

This is the Kenmar Road exit in Fortuna, located next to a levee. Water from the broken levee traveled all the way up to Fortuna Boulevard, which is uphill about a quarter mile away.

Here, water creeps toward Fortuna Boulevard, carrying tons of debris with it. The Highway 101 overpass shows the depth of the water.

This photograph was shot just north of the Twelfth Street break and shows the Twelfth Street overpass. The flooded area is Highway 101.

In a view looking north on Highway 101 at the Twelfth Street overpass, one sees Clendenen's apple orchard on the right. Note the logs and other items on the highway.

In this view looking south on Highway 101, one sees the Pacific Lumber Company mill on the left.

This view, looking south onto South Twelfth Street, depicts a destroyed bridge. It was pummeled with redwood logs, which are seen everywhere. The crane in the background tried to save the bridge from the logjam.

In a view looking south from Highway 101, the Twelfth Street overpass is a good place to see how big these logs are that washed downriver. The Pacific Lumber mill is seen in the background.

# *Four*

# VAN DUZEN RIVER AND ALTON

This view is looking west at the intersection of Highway 36 and Highway 101. Note the large logs in the freeway.

Pictured is the Old West Trading Post at the intersection of Highway 36 and Highway 101. The floodwaters had picked the building up and rotated it. After the water went down, the building was salvaged and was there until 2010.

The Van Duzen River is seen here going over the dike at Alton. The dikes were put into place after the 1955 flood; many thought the water would not get that high again.

The US Army deployed amphibious vehicles to aid in the rescue of stranded homeowners. Here, they are crossing the railroad tracks into Alton.

Here, the Van Duzen River has risen all the way up into the town of Alton. This view is looking south from Highway 36.

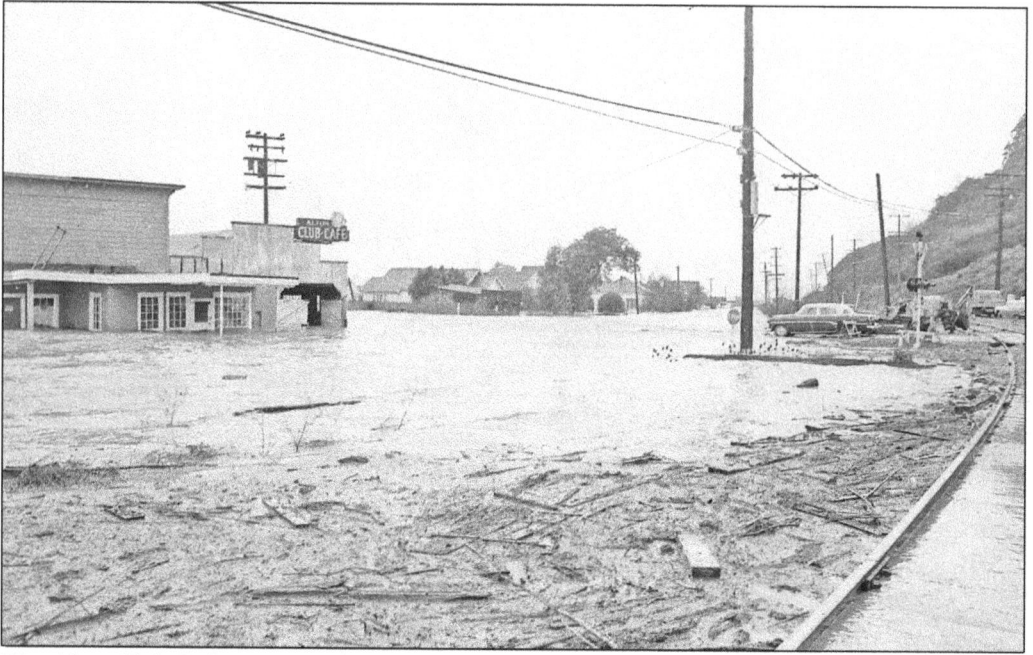

The Alton Club Cafe is seen on the left with about three feet of water inside. The bar was reopened shortly after and remained a favorite watering hole for many years after.

This aerial view shows the logjam at Van Duzen River Bridge. There were several mills upstream that lost their log decks, which wound up here at the mouth of the river.

Henry and Alaris Cardoza's dairy ranch is seen in the center, and Hector Senestraro's ranch is at the top center of photograph. At one point, the Cardozas' ranch looked like an island with water reaching their doorsteps. Luckily, no water entered their house.

Rescue personnel have a boat full of evacuees being taken to higher ground. Lee Woodcock is seen at the front of the boat with a hood on.

This US Army amphibious vehicle makes its way down Highway 36 down toward Highway 101.

A local Alton resident is making a break for it with his boat. Many people were glad that they at least had their boats when the water kept rising.

This aerial view shows the reality of the flood at the confluence of the Van Duzen and Eel Rivers. Ferndale is in the background underwater. Between these two rivers, a record was set for the volume and amount of sediment flushed downriver.

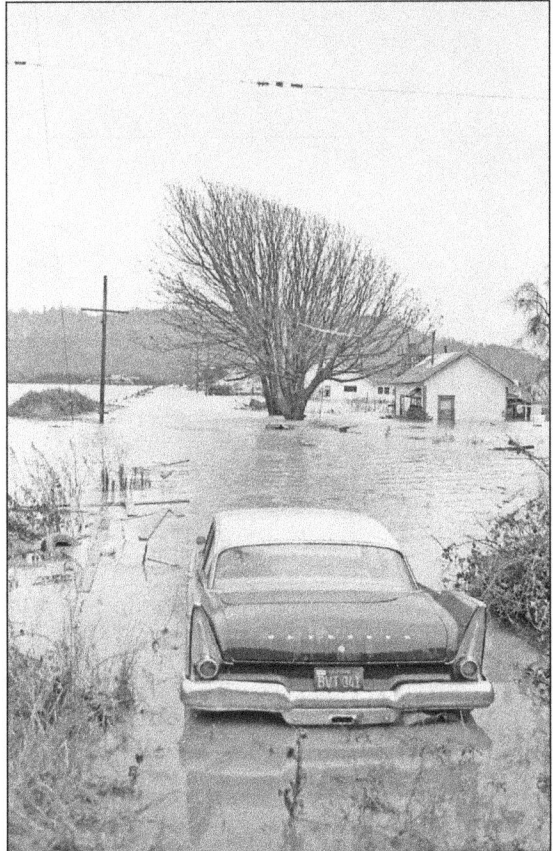

This old Plymouth sits abandoned in the floodwaters at Alton.

The Van Duzen Grange is completely flooded from rising Yager Creek.

This looks like a river, but it is actually Yager Creek flowing into the Van Duzen River. Tons of logs and debris helped clutter the already overflowing Van Duzen River.

Here, an observer looks at the logjam being created at Yager Creek.

This aerial view, looking east, shows the Starvation Flat area along the Van Duzen River after the water started to recede. Most homes were completely destroyed.

Snakes were one of the many hidden perils of the flood. Pictured is a harmless California king snake; however, rattlesnakes were also found along the Van Duzen and the Eel Rivers logjams.

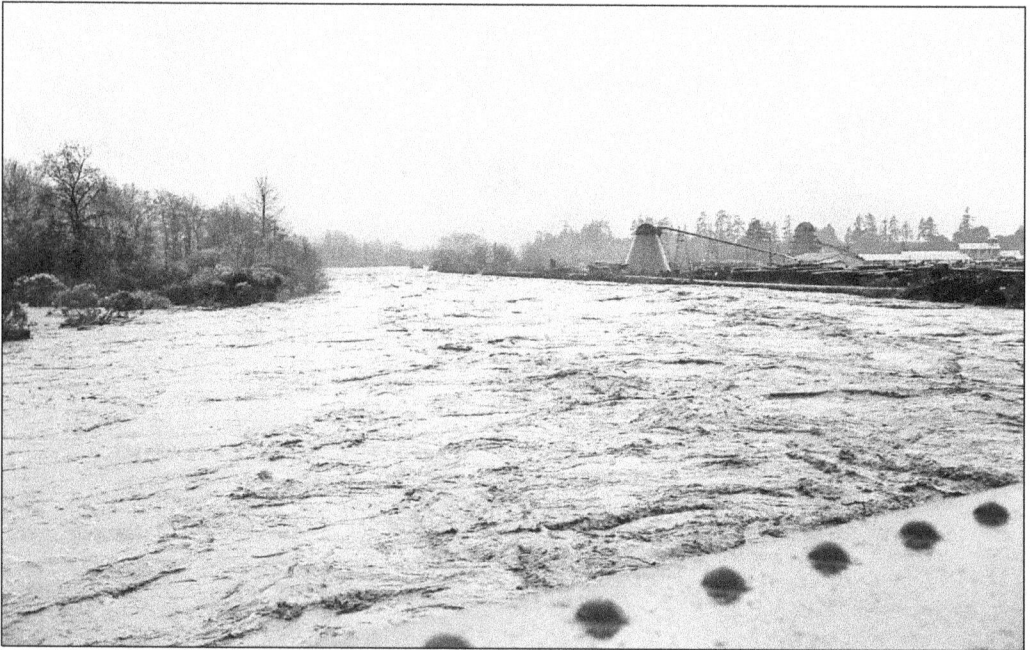

Looking north up Yager Creek, this view shows an unbelievable amount of water coming down this once docile creek.

This view of Sandy Prairie shows just how high the water had risen with the Van Duzen River adding 40,000 cubic feet square to the already raging Eel River. Note the gap in the dike at top right of photograph; it indicates where the dike broke.

In this view looking northwest over the town of Alton, all that is visible is water. Once the Van Duzen flowed into the Eel River, nothing could hold back this volume of water.

This view is looking south toward Alton; the homes and ranches are still there today. Here, the water was about five to six feet deep at its peak. Note the railroad tracks to the right of the trees.

This is a close-up of the previous image. Note the depth of the water on the house and the City of Fortuna's water pumping station. This is the present-day area of the Fortuna's gun club's skeet shooting range.

This view from the bluffs in Campton Heights looks over Sandy Prairie. When the water went over the dikes at Alton and Fortuna, it inundated these low-lying areas. Today, the area is known for its wonderful strawberries in part due to the fertile silt left by the flood.

In this view looking south toward Alton, one can see the Humboldt Drive-in. This area by Drake Hill Road was under several feet of water but was saved from total destruction because it sits on a small knoll, located away from the current of the Eel and Van Duzen Rivers.

This was a common scene along the Eel River valley. The ranches were underwater, and there is no sign of any animal. Many cows were saved only to wander back out to deep water and be swept downriver. One cow actually wound up in Crescent City totally unharmed and was returned to its owner.

A ranch house and barn sit deep in water along the Eel River; this property was one of the first casualties of the dike breaking at South Twelfth Street where River Lodge sits today. Again, no animals are seen. Downstream, there were dead cows everywhere, and some ranchers lost their whole herds and were forced out of business.

Looking toward Drake Hill, the view in this photograph shows logs and telephone poles everywhere. Today, one can find a skeet shooting range and strawberry fields in this area.

The telltale sign of the depth of the water is the silt marking on the house; this home was remodeled and is still there today.

This home was located along Sandy Prairie, and as with most houses, it was torn down and rebuilt because the silt got into every nook and cranny. It was next to impossible to clean out.

Hansen's wire rope and the Humboldt Drive-in were located on Highway 101. In the photograph, there is a misplaced roof on the side of the road.

*Five*

# RIO DELL AND SCOTIA

Rudy Gillard took this photograph just as the bridge fell. Not pictured is the car driven by a Dr. Tredwell; the doctor had just cleared the span on an emergency call to deliver a baby when the bridge fell into the Eel River. California Highway Patrol had tried to stop him but failed.

Once the fog cleared, the total destruction of the Paul Mudgett Bridge was visible to all. The bridge spanned the Eel River north of the town of Rio Dell. During the flood, the town of Rio Dell lost both northbound and southbound bridges, making it landlocked.

The beautiful Mozetti ranch serves as a backdrop to the destroyed remains of the railroad tracks that passed through the canyon along Rio Dell. This whole section of tracks was washed out along the Scotia and Rio Dell bluffs. To get the rail system back up and running was one of the area's first priorities. Note the riprap that was poured to try to save the tracks.

This amazing photograph really shows the destruction in Metropolitan, which is just north of Rio Dell. Pictured are the remains of the bridge in Rio Dell and some homes. Several of these houses still exist today.

This image is identical to the previous photograph of Metropolitan, but the river is almost back to its normal height. The buildings pictured were at one time used as a seminary and school; today, the Bravo family members use them as their private homes.

A view looking south toward the town of Rio Dell shows what was left of the Eel River Sawmill. The curve in the river was an ideal spot for all the debris to pile up at; it was also the spot where several home came to rest.

A Cessna plane lands on Wildwood Avenue, also known as at the "Rio Dell Airport." It was the only way to get much-needed supplies into this small town cut off from the rest of the world.

Here is the Paul Mudgett Bridge on the north side of Rio Dell, with Mozetti ranch in the distance. The home office of the Eel River Sawmill survived the flood and is still standing today.

This is a closer view showing the property and main office of the Eel River Sawmill. This area became a graveyard for several homes that piled up against the off-ramp of the Paul Mudgett Bridge.

Pictured are Metropolitan, Rio Dell, and the remains of the Eel River Sawmill; this wide-angle view really gives an idea of how wide the raging Eel River got when it was at full force.

This photograph was taken from the opposite direction of the last photograph and was clearly taken after the water went down. Mel McLean, owner of Eel River Sawmill, was determined to rebuild his prized mill and went on to do so in record time.

This is what Mel McLean got to see firsthand of his prized lumber mill. Being the owner of the operation, he was always thinking about his employees who relied on him and went ahead with full force to recover what was left of his log deck and units of lumber that were strewn about for mile and miles. It appears that several home and businesses floated intact to this location.

Here, the recovery project is underway at the Eel River Sawmill. One can see that the log deck is being restacked, and units of lumber that were recovered are being put in some sort of order. It is hard to believe that this mill was actually put back in working order in no time at all.

Here is the sawmill after a full recovery from the flood. A lot of hard work by a ton of people was put into the sawmill. This mill provided hundreds of well-paying jobs in Humboldt County.

After the floodwaters receded, these banded units of Douglas fir were found sitting in place at the mill yard. Also, the main office was left intact.

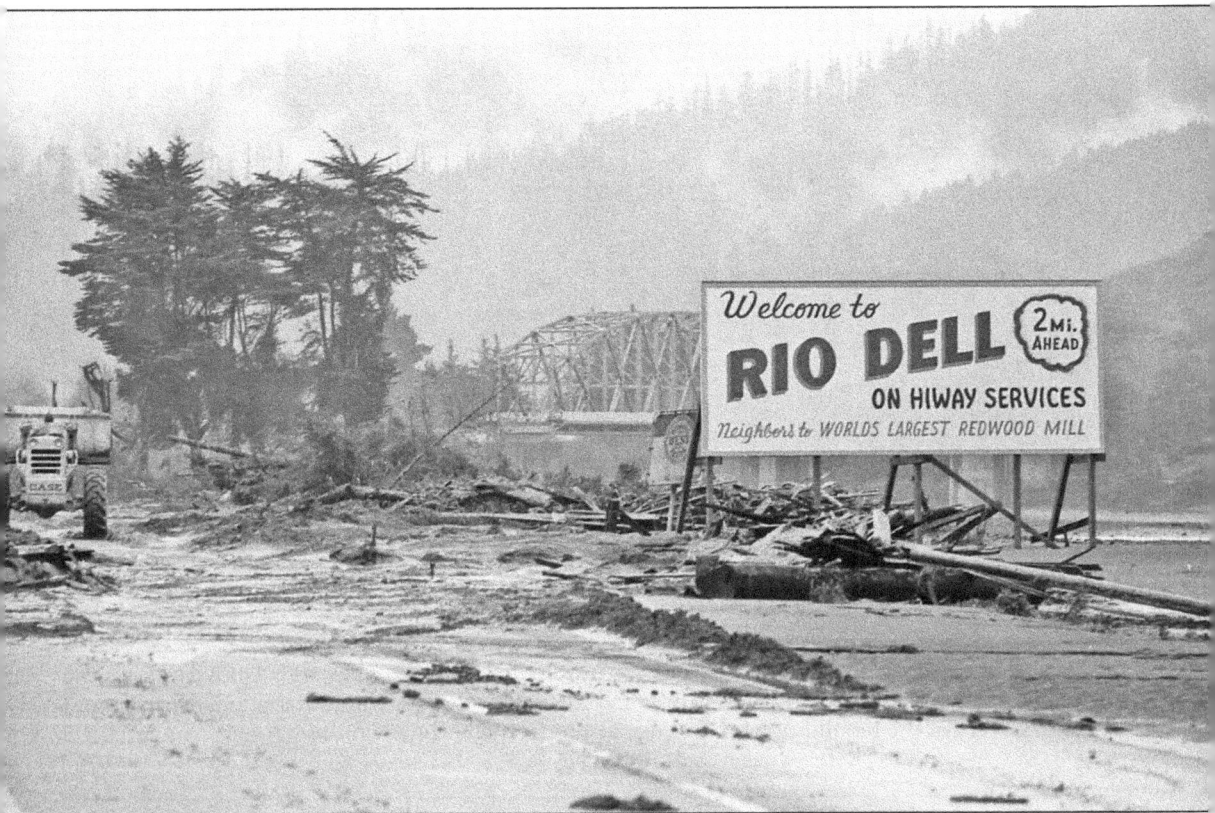

Amidst all the destruction, this sign withstood the powerful force of the Eel River. The remains of the Paul Mudgett Bridge are seen in the distance. In order for work crews to get busy rebuilding the bridge, a Case loader was used to aid in the removal of all the debris that blocked access to the span.

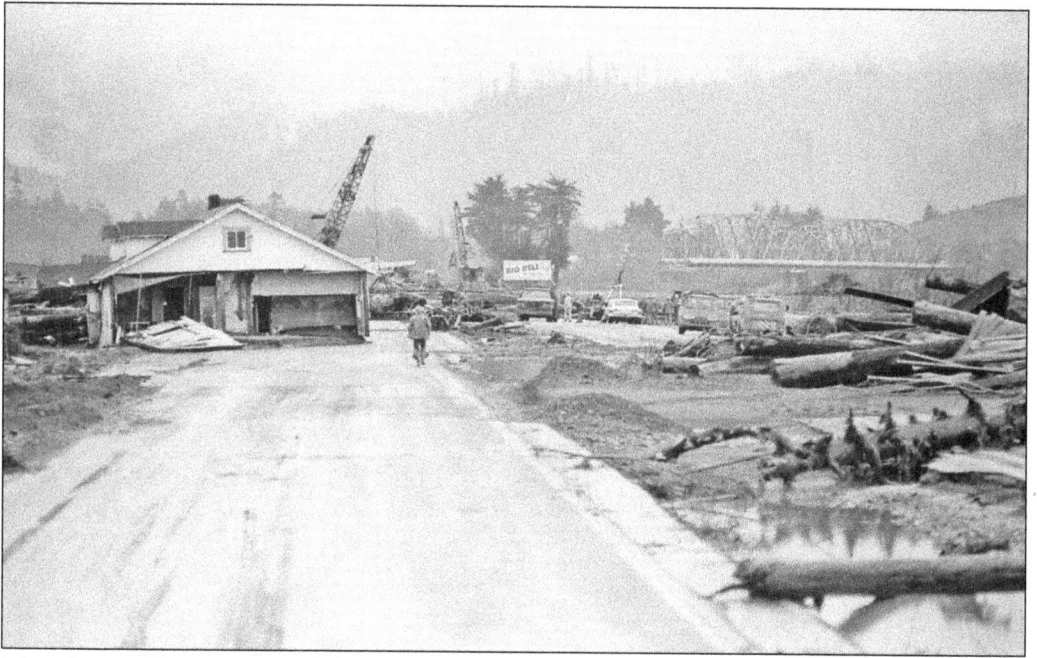

Many homes that were carried downriver were pretty much intact when they landed right in the middle of Highway 101 across the way from Eel River Sawmill. This large amount of debris slowed the recovery of the rebuilding of the bridge at Rio Dell and the sawmill.

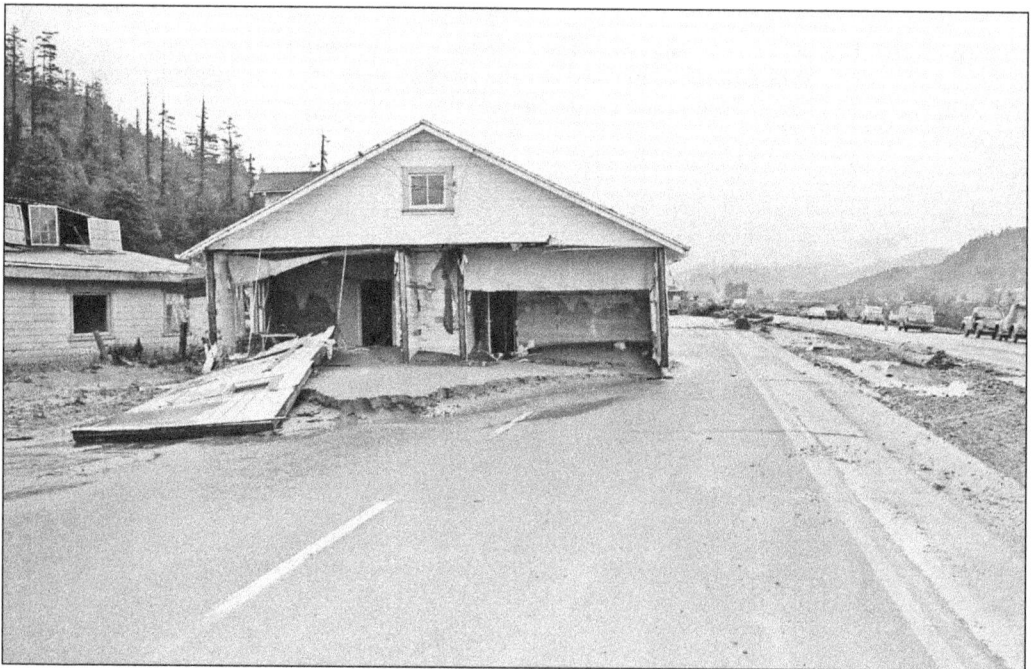

The homes that floated downriver intact must have been well built to be able withstand the powerful forces of this flood. Back then, most home were constructed with tongue-and-groove lumber (redwood or Douglas fir) from the local mills.

This was one of many businesses that came from miles away upstream mostly intact. One can see the boom from a tow truck buried in lumber along with many wrapped Christmas presents.

Most of the structures were built to last, which is evident by the barn on the left that appears to be untouched by the floodwaters. Note in the top right there is a structure hanging on the edge of this crumbling cliff.

Pictured is Metropolitan after the water receded. The Bravo family, who still lives there today, owns the home on the left, and the large structure was a seminary at one time. Hunts Dairy at the top right was situated on higher ground and was spared by the floodwaters. As one can see, logs were everywhere.

These two men are looking for what was left of their Christmas presents and remarkably Robert Knapp Sr. found not only a lost toy tractor but also his wife's purse. The force of the water flipped logging truck like little toys.

This home met its fate at the off-ramp of the Paul Mudgett Bridge north of Rio Dell. The river cut a new channel and headed toward Metropolitan and Eel River Sawmill, wreaking havoc in its wake.

Along with fixed-wing airplanes, military and private helicopters were used to ferry in supplies to locations like Rio Dell, which was landlocked. So many people who owned such craft stepped up to the plate to help however they could.

The silt from the Eel River trapped this large crane at the log deck at Eel River Sawmill. The fields around Southern Humboldt County are some of the richest farmlands anywhere because of all the silt that was deposited by the flood.

A stark reminder of the date of the disaster is depicted in this photograph as some little girl's Christmas present is seen covered in mud. There was an outpouring of help by the local communities to replace children's presents and to help them deal with this horrible event.

This photograph shows Pacific Lumber Company housing along the Eel River. The whole row of homes was lost along with a large portion of old-growth redwood logs that were sitting in a log deck adjacent to the river. The structure on the left was Bertain's laundry, which today is the wood shop for the mill.

Here, the Pacific Lumber Company's drying kilns are almost underwater from the rising Eel River. Thankfully, the river spared the millions of board feet of precious old-growth redwood located inside. Unfortunately, the river did not spare the log deck and other areas of the world's largest redwood mill. Also note the flipped railroad boxcar sitting in the river.

The truck shop, located adjacent to Highway 101, was also flooded. The Pacific Lumber Company owned it, and since it was a sturdy structure, it survived the pounding river and is still in use today.

One of the hardest-hit industries was the Northwestern Pacific Railroad, which took a pounding, as it lost hundreds of railcars and mile after mile of railroad tracks on the 100-plus-mile train route that paralleled the Eel River.

This photograph was taken out of the front window of the main office of the Pacific Lumber Company. Helicopters were helpful in transporting much-needed supplies to the towns that were cut off.

Fireman's Park in the town of Scotia is seen inundated by tons of debris. It is amazing that such small trees withstood the unbelievable force of the river, especially since redwood trees have shallow root systems, making them vulnerable to falling over.

# Six

# MAIN EEL IN SOUTHERN HUMBOLDT

Locally known as the South Scotia Bridge, this structure was dedicated January 10, 1917, as a final section of the highway linking Eureka to San Francisco. The two-lane bridge just downstream was built in 1961, and despite the protection from debris from the old bridge, the new structure was washed out. A sharp eye can pick out a tree lodged in the framework of the old bridge on the right.

Among all the picture-taking of the South Scotia Bridge, only one photographer walked up the south portal and took a picture of the tree in the framework of the structure. The horizontal bracing inside the bridge made it so narrow that the side-view mirrors on two passing trucks would hit each other. The narrow width was also the cause of many accidents.

The village of Stafford was almost completely covered with water. At the top left is the South Scotia Bridge. Near center of the photograph and behind the Thompson house is an empty water tank on top of a 20-foot-high redwood stump. Cut off from the evacuation, Don and Rose Thompson spent the whole night of December 22 in the empty water tank.

This is a close-up of the water tank in the last picture. The water tank was held in high esteem after the floodwaters receded. Many times during the night of the December 22, debris struck the stump and tank, and Don and Rose Thompson were well aware that the next piece of drift could crush the tank or push it off the stump; however, they survived that harrowing night.

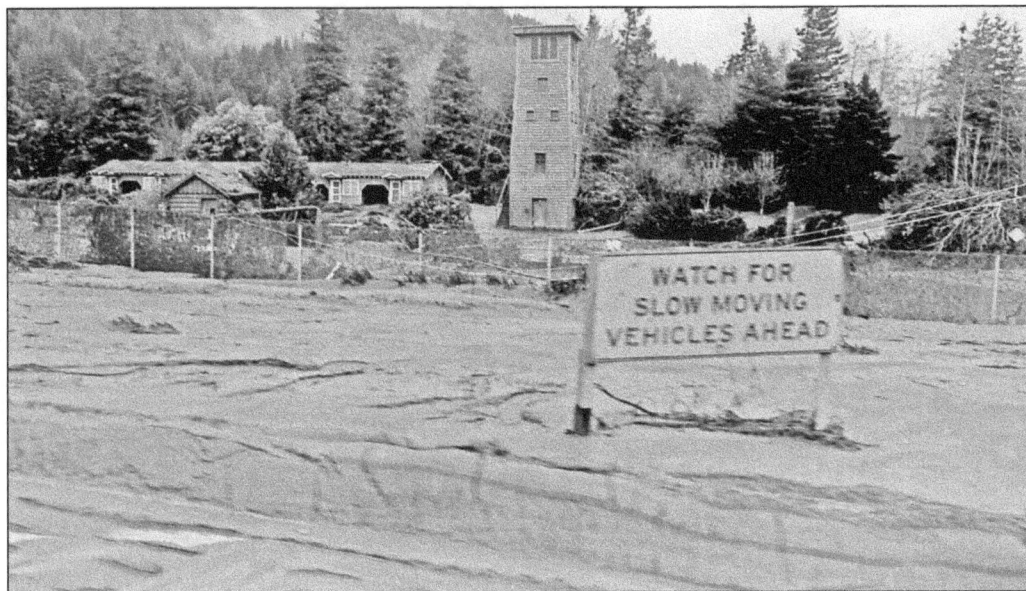

Located in the north end of Stafford at the south portal of the South Scotia Bridge was the site of the Browers' Motel, also known as the "Eel River Motel" or the "Tower Motel." There was a lot of damage to the motel, as well as a tangle of power lines, because that area was the collection point for the debris from the village.

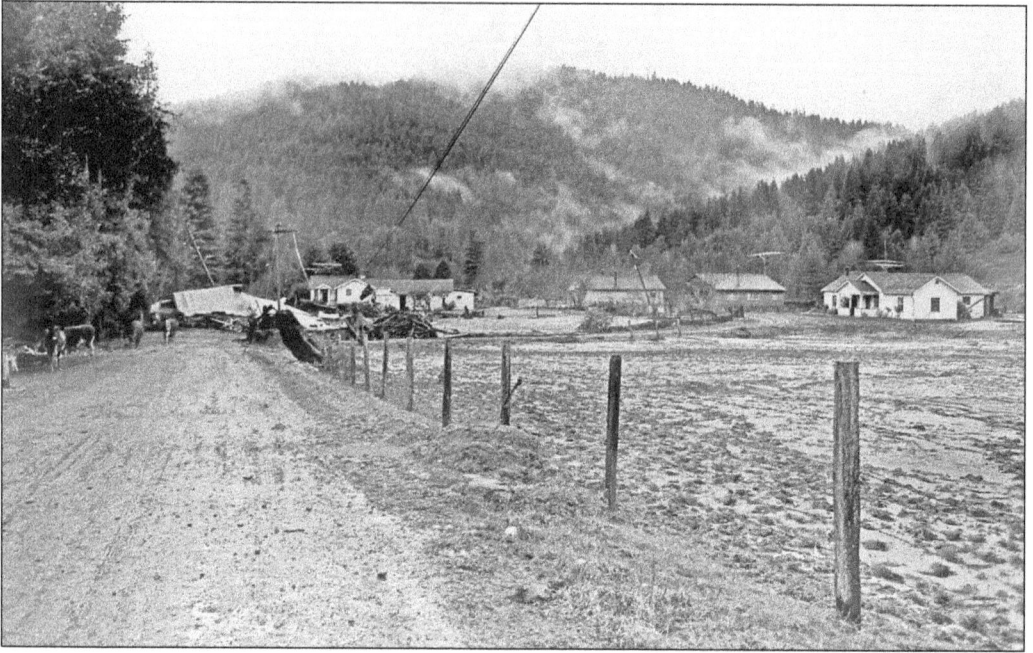

Central Stafford along the original highway was close to the river. Damage was heavy, and enough mud covered the grazing fields that cattle could not feed. On the old road in the middle left, four cattle are wandering in search of food. The few ranchers who did have feed were quick to share with others not so lucky. Efforts by civil disaster agencies soon brought feed for cattle, as well as for people.

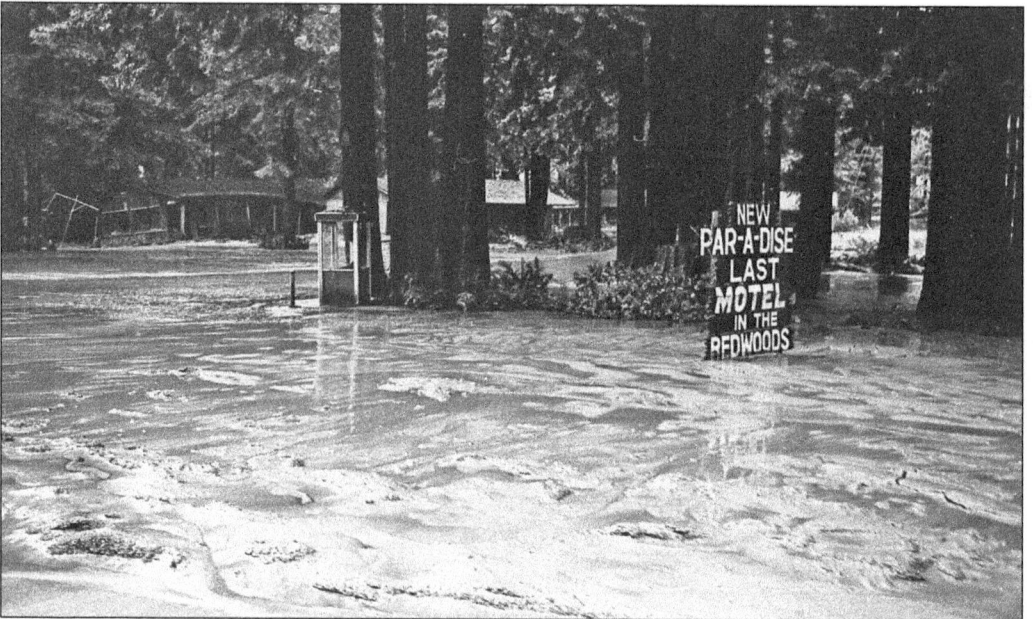

Just north of Pepperwood was Dillon's Par-a-dise Motel. The sign says new because the motel was nearly destroyed in the 1955 flood. In addition to the cabins were an upscale restaurant, a gift shop, and a 23-foot-wide drive-through stump, which was also lost in the flood of 1955.

82

Between Par-a-dise Motel and Pepperwood was a small group of houses. Most were rentals for employees of the timber industry. Though the site was on higher ground than Dillon's Par-a-dise Motel and Pepperwood and the trees blocked the main force of the current, only one house survived the flood. It was pushed against the tree line on the downstream side of the clearing. On the right side of the image, salvaged clothing can be seen hanging on a makeshift line.

This photograph was taken during the first of many flyovers of Pepperwood; it depicts a few hours after the crest, sometime in the late morning of December 23. Seen on the right are most of the town's buildings piled up against a row of redwoods, which were planted by "Papa" St. John several years before. In the center are more houses piled up against another row of trees where the Flood Plain produce stand is today. Directly to the left is another set of buildings piled up against a grove of trees where the corncrib stand is today. Similar images to this one were front-page news all over the United States.

Just to the right of the Angus Russell house was a motel that had survived the 1937 flood, the 1955 flood, and now the 1964 flood. The Cottage Court was a popular stopping place in the 1940s. No one was quite sure why the buildings stayed as they were in the lowest part of Pepperwood. A fair-sized tree is on one of the unit, and it serves a silent testimony to the sturdiness of these buildings.

In a view moving south of that in the previous photograph, this is the main pileup of most of the houses in Pepperwood. A row of planted, small second-growth redwoods managed to hold most of the debris from upstream. An engineer flying over made the comment that these small redwoods withstood more force than what took out most of the highway bridges.

Continuing south past the Angus Russell home, Boehm's restaurant can be seen on its side. This was the heart of Pepperwood and was where most of the buildings came to rest. None of these buildings were salvageable, so owners took what they could and moved on.

In Pepperwood, there were two traditional places of safety. The first was the water tower by the school, and second was Van Noys restaurant. Van Noys was chosen to be evacuated because there were so many people at the restaurant. Albert Porter began taking people out four at a time and made several trips to safety. In the last trip to the restaurant, the water was too swift, and big drift was hitting the boat, nearly capsizing it. Albert had to turn away; his wife, Florence, was one of the five who drowned.

In the center of the picture is Pete's Grocery, a survivor of the 1955 flood. At the southern part of town, the store was on the only highway turn in town. Behind the store is the one surviving house, out of three in the area. On the other side of the highway were Babe Millsap's Mobil station and De Fries Shell station, which were destroyed. At the bottom right is the old Lucas Hotel, which was converted to the Garcia residence.

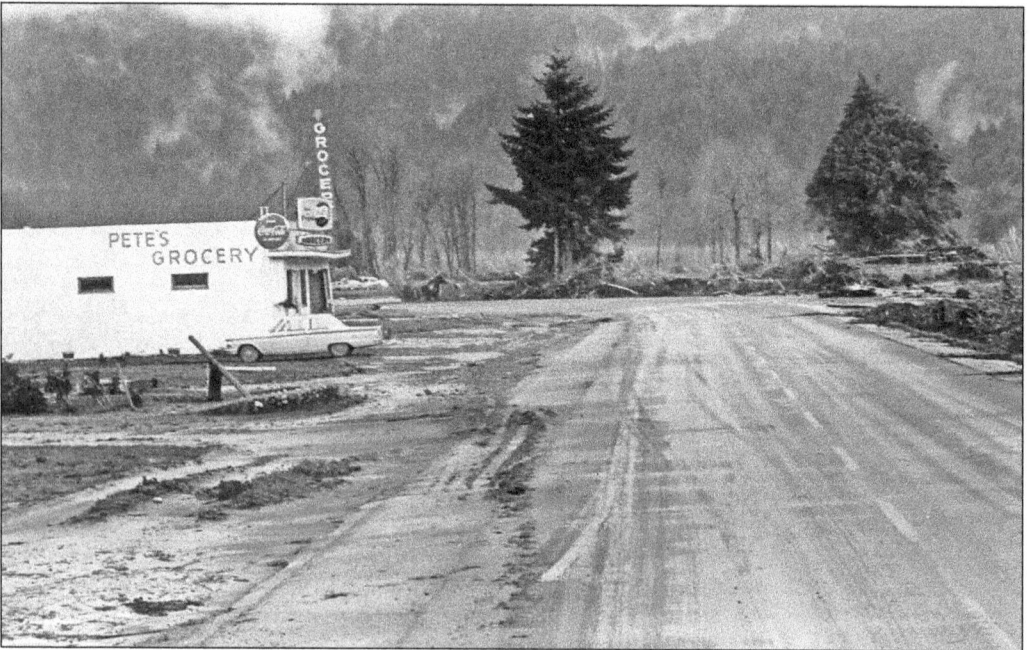

Pete's Grocery after the water subsided was a disaster inside. Most of the inventory that stayed in the building was scattered, broken, or saturated with silt. The Pepperwood turn area was the heart of the business district. Almost all the structures were swept away because of the swift current. Cleanup in the area was mostly throwing away of what was left.

Here is a close-up the Garcia home. The front was torn away, and a couple of feet of silt deposited on the bottom floor. A social center around the turn of the century, this structure was the Lucas Hotel. A major attraction was the world's largest pepperwood tree growing behind the building.

Another of the many popular photographs was of the Pacific Lumber Company barn from Larabee, three miles upstream. Caught in a thick pile of drift, the hay inside stayed dry and was an important source of food for livestock. On the left side of the barn is the Bee Tree, a popular stopping place on the path to the swimming hole. The swimming hole was filled in by the flood and abandoned.

One of the few pictures made of Shively was a flyover taken by college student David Carneggie, who came up to salvage what was possible out of his parents' store, Pete's Grocery. David donated this photograph to the flood collection. His second job was to guide his professors from the University of California, Berkeley, who were studying flood damage and siltation in the park. Almost the whole bottom of Shively next to the river was swept clean.

Just south of Bear Creek, the highway not only suffered flooding but also a large slide of fill from the new freeway under construction. Fill was brought down from Horse Collar Creek to the lower ground above Bear Creek. This fill was made up of old river run rock and gravel and was unusable. In the background, neighbors are trying to help a stuck vehicle.

This aerial of Holmes was probably taken late on the morning of December 23. Two-thirds of all structures were totally destroyed at first estimates, but later inspections claimed many more. All the cattle were saved by a night drive up an old logging road to Englewood. Many community members were taken into the only three homes not flooded, and the rest were taken in by neighboring communities.

The Stockel house, which had recently been built, was caught in a cluster of redwoods in the schoolyard. In this area, all the homes, the Grange hall, and school were swept away. Most washed against the redwood forest at the north end of the valley. One of the homes in the area broke up, and a bowling trophy from inside was found on Loleta bottoms some 35 miles downstream.

A few yards from the Stockel house was Stockton Farm. The water came up so fast that there was no time to get the cars to high ground. As a comparison of the two floods at the Stockton home, the level was three feet deep in 1955 and almost 13 feet in the 1964 flood. There was six inches of mud upstairs and almost three feet downstairs. The house was pushed hard by the current, but thanks to Gene Mcarthy, the builder, it stayed together.

The Evans house was built piece by piece by Jerry Evans. A tree faller by trade, Jerry was highly skilled in all types of building. In the summer of 1964, Jerry and his wife Flora sold the place and moved to town. After the flood, the people who bought the house from Jerry left for good, so Jerry cleaned it up, developed a fine orchard, and in a few years, sold it again.

Due east of Holmes is the community of Larabee. In its brief past, this area had several logging camps with railroads that reached 12 miles into the backcountry. Shown here is the Larabee lodge owned by the Pacific Lumber Company. Damage to the lodge was severe but not total.

The county bridge over Larabee Creek was not terribly damaged. The cables had slipped off the top due to drift lifting the bridge. It appeared that all that was needed was to slip the cables over the top piers again and all would be well. An attempt to do this failed, and the bridge fell to the ground below.

The railroad south of the Evans ranch was undermined for several hundred yards. Ray Evans and his brother Arthur walked down these tracks the night before the tracks were lost. That evacuation night, the ranch was 40 acres, and the next day, it was four acres of mud and silt. Parts of the house remained, as well as a huge barn built by Ray's older brother Jerry.

The South Fork Railroad Bridge was completed in 1910. There was a severe flood in 1915 that destroyed all the highway bridges except the Dyerville and Fernbridge Bridges. In 1937, the Eel River flooded again and stayed high for a long period of time. The bridge survived again in the 1955 flood when the water was near the tracks. In 1964, the water was 10 feet over the tracks, which made its depth about 80 feet.

The southern end of South Fork shows a tangle of railcars that resemble scatted toys. Many houses seen in the upper right of the photograph were destroyed, but most of the structures on the middle right were washed away or piled up in the woods at Founders Grove. This was the business area of the village.

Along the tree line of the southern border was a continuous line of drift, including buildings, cars, and about everything else in the community. The Standard Oil warehouse was pushed a few hundred yards north and was torn apart by the river. When the silt was dry enough to walk on, debris was found scattered several hundred yard into the woods.

The Flying A and the Texaco gas distributors suffered the same fate as the Standard Oil company. Just to the right of the Dyerville Loop Road was a hollow where many of South Fork structures—as well as 20,000 to 30,000 gallons of gasoline—came to rest. The whole of South Fork was quarantined for six weeks.

## Seven

# SOUTH FORK EEL IN SOUTHERN HUMBOLDT

The next town upstream from Larabee was Dyerville. It had been wiped away in the 1955 flood, and all that was left was a bridge. Built in 1934, Dyerville Bridge was on the main Highway 101 artery until a four-lane bridge was built beside it in 1957. About 10 hours after this photograph was taken, a 12-foot-diameter redwood tree slid into the bridge and measured about a third of its length. The tree was caught while debris accumulated on its root wad until enough force lifted the whole bridge off its piers.

Here is another view of the Dyerville Bridge from the freeway bridge. Ray Evans from Larabee walked with his brother to this vantage point and saw a five-foot-diameter redwood log hit this span flush on the framework. In a few seconds, tremendous pressure built up, and the log broke in half. Everyone there was in disbelief as the two halves were sucked under the bridge with the rest of the debris.

The next morning, Robert Childs drove down the freeway to check on the river. Robert took this picture from the freeway bridge. The old bridge was so full of debris that it floated about 200 yards downstream and came to rest on the riverbank. The framework was bent and twisted beyond all recognition. Robert also donated his photographs to the 1964 flood collection.

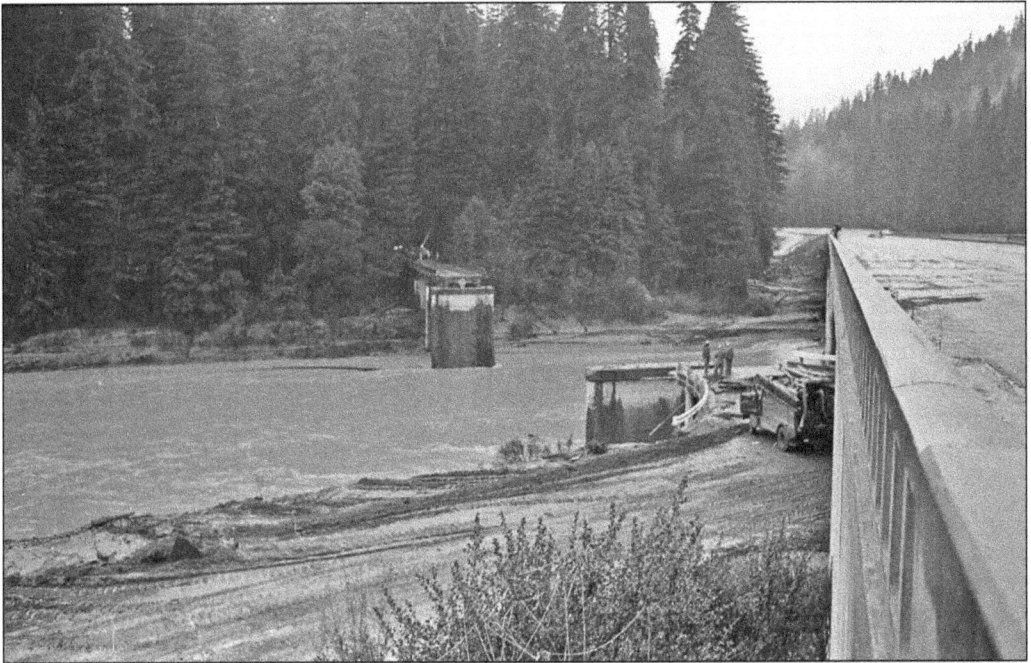

Pacific Gas and Electric crews moved in quickly to shoot a line across the river to replace the one that was lost inside the bridge. The telephone company did the same with their lines, and so did the water company with its waterlines in Founders Grove. Later, all the lines were put in the new two-lane bridge, which was built two years later.

Sometime after the water receded, Dyerville flat became a staging area for construction equipment and supplies needed for restoration and recovery. Repairs needed to be done to the railroad, highways, and towns. The lumber industry also began operations again.

At the south end of the freeway, Robin Childs looks upstream toward the Federation overpass. The on-ramp lights were cut down to enable small aircraft to land on the freeway bridge. Supplies and people were brought in and taken out for several days. One pilot lived in Redcrest, so he would taxi up the freeway four miles to his home every night.

The four-lane bridge at Dyerville barely escaped the fate of the two-lane bridge. Drift piled under and against this new bridge and lifted the whole center span a foot off its piers. Two alert highway workers, Jim Chaley and William Wilson (seen in the photograph) dropped two charges of dynamite that began a spreading of the drift, enabling it to go under the bridge safely.

As the water was receding, photographer Rudy Gillard did a flyover of the Eel River Canyon. At Dyerville, drift is on the freeway that would soon be cleared for air traffic. In the middle left, the two-lane bridge approach can seen coming out of Founders Grove.

The freeway bridge at Dyerville was covered with water on the south end. By December 23, the water had receded enough for Caltrans crews to clear the debris. The "Dyerville airport" was born, and small airplanes landing here established a link with the outside world. Richard Bullock, a contract pilot with California Division of Forestry, was the main pilot bringing people in and out for several weeks.

This aerial shows the whole town of Weott to the new freeway and above. After the 1955 flood, people began to relocate and build on higher ground, thinking for sure that the Eel River could not pass the 17-foot level on the old highway. In 1964, the depth on the old highway was over 33 feet. This picture, probably taken December 23, is after the crest, with the water down to about the 1955 level.

Here is a composite view of the sea of mud deposited by the river in central Weott. The bulldozer along with a bucket loader, operated by John Milligan, was trying to clear the highway and entrances to structures. Several passes were required to clear a path. About 20 feet left from the right-hand light pole is Don Archers's sawhorse straddling the telephone wire.

Traveling down the freeway off-ramp, the water on the road accesses the old highway. A victim of both water and mud, the Weott Christian Church was unsalvageable. On the back left, Cathy's Café was destroyed a second time. Left of Cathy's Café was the post office, which ended upside down.

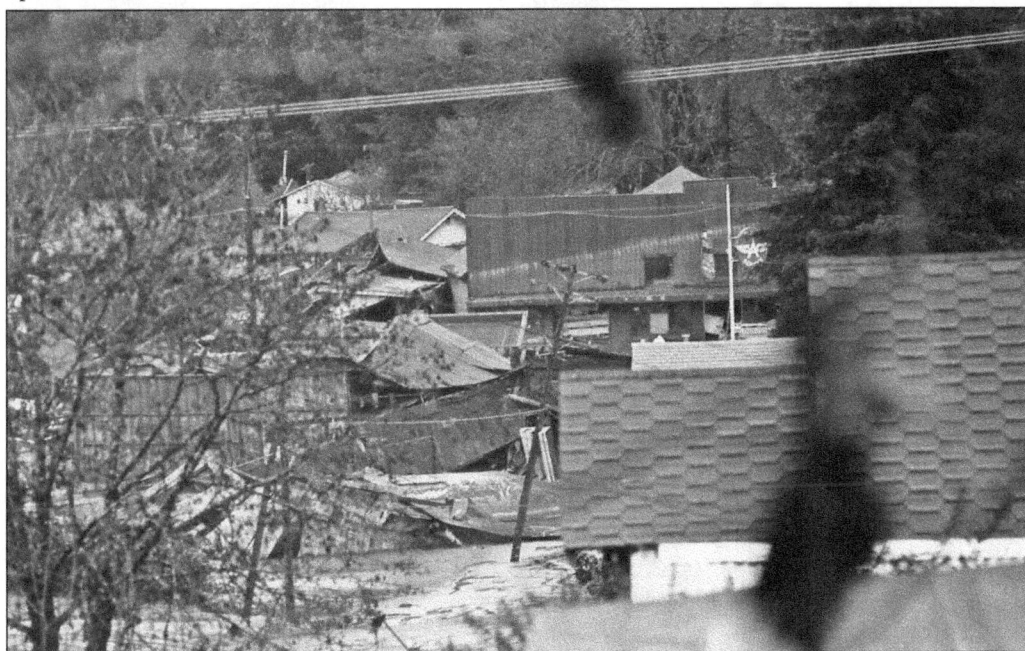

In the center of the picture just behind the Flying A sign is Johnson's store. The watermark left by the river shows the building was tilted, so it was held fast. Damage here was so severe that the store was relocated above the new floodplain, which is just about where this picture was taken. Most of the businesspeople were not going to tempt the river a third time.

This photograph of Weott was taken several days after the flood peak. The building at the bottom right (the Legion hall) was well above the floodplain, and its location became a new place to build since it was safe from the river. Nearly all the buildings on the flat were burned the next summer.

As with many communities along the river, high ground was sought for shelter, and people evacuated with their automobiles and everything worth carrying out of homes and businesses. The Agnes Johnson School fit this purpose and became the civil defense headquarters.

In the months that followed, buildings in each community were inspected, and the red-circle X meant the structure was beyond repair. This house near Weott is being piled up to burn by contractor Jim Wheeler, a logger pressed into service to help with the massive cleanup.

The small town of Myers Flat was a mill town. Hard-hit in 1955, the Morrison-Jackson Mill and the business district were rebuilt. In 1964, logs and lumber piled up on the north end of town. Don Quinn's residence is almost alone on the lower flat.

A closer look at the north end of town shows lumber piled up against a tree line bordering the river. This pileup of lumber and logs saved a lot of structures downstream. Everything in this pileup was lost except the Drive-Thru Tree. On the upper left, the drive-in screen survived.

Here is another view of the Morison-Jackson Mill with the current flowing to the north part of town. The top building on the right was the town Laundromat, and tradition has it the river peaked on its second step. Just to the right and out of the picture is the Myers Inn, where the 1862 flood level was at the floor about four feet higher.

This is the north end of Myers Flat seen from the highway. Most businesses were destroyed in this area. A massive cleanup with heavy equipment was needed just to open the highway. A bulldozer is seen here removing lumber that was damaged beyond salvaging. Later, it was burned.

The new freeways played an important part in saving vehicles and other equipment. When people had a short time to choose what was to be saved, almost everyone chose pictures, keepsakes, and things with emotional attachment.

Between Myers Flat and Salmon Creek was a low place in the new freeway, just dedicated the year before. A narrow gorge in this area forced the water high up on the banks. Several houses were seen floating downstream from here that met their destruction on the Dyerville Bridge.

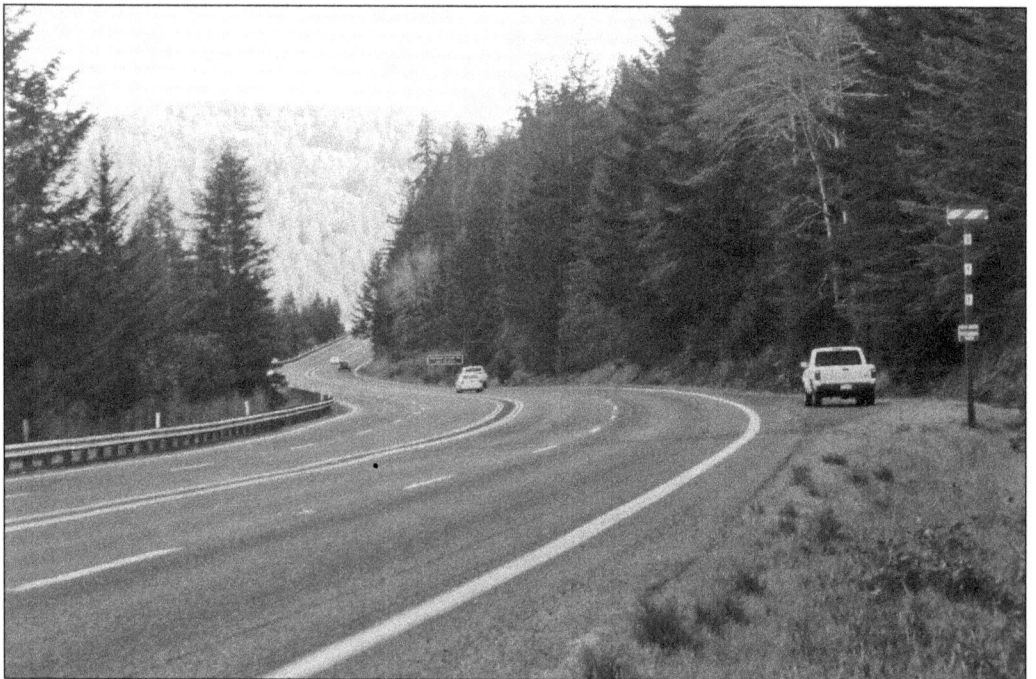

This section of freeway was never filled to be above the 1964 flood level. The highway department installed a series of high-watermark signs by some of the flooded towns. This one shows the water to be 15 feet deep over the freeway.

Boyd Creek on the north end of Phillipsville had its channel gutted by the huge volume of water runoff. Gravel was over five feet deep on the Avenue of the Giants and parts of Phillipsville. State park officials are assessing damage to Franklin K. Lane Grove that includes part of the Boyd Creek watershed.

The town of Phillipsville had a low part by the river and a higher part above the floodplain. The freeway was on the opposite side of town, but there were roads and a hill that enabled residents to access safe places to evacuate. As with other towns in the area, there was heavy damage to most of the village.

Benbow State Recreation area enjoys popularity as a destination and vacation spot. As seen here, not only flooding but also erosion caused heavy damage to the landscape. In the background is the famous Benbow Inn, a popular place for movie stars in the 1940s.

The bridge over the South Fork of the Eel next to the town of Redway was completely destroyed. Damage to both approaches was severe and was caused by the undermining of several large redwood trees that fell on the framing. All of the spans were torn off the piers and were beyond salvaging.

# *Eight*

# RECOVERY BEGINS

The USS *Bennington* aircraft carrier waits offshore Humboldt Bay; it was used in the rescue and relief effort during the flood.

This photograph shows the completed railroad bridge on the South Fork of the Eel River. Every effort was made to get the railroad completed to aid in reconstruction after the flood. The rail system brought in most of the supplies needed to rebuild.

This image shows the replacement for the bridge that was swept down the South Fork of the Eel River. The new bridge was built in sections just in case of catastrophic events like this: The middle section will wash out to relieve the stress on the rest of the bridge.

The main street of Rio Dell became an airstrip to bring in supplies because the bridges on both ends of town were washed out, making Rio Dell landlocked.

This photograph shows Jack Epping bulldozing down his own home, which he spent nights and weekends remodeling for two years prior to the flood. The house was built in 1911, and his wife, Marion, as well as the book's coauthor's mother, Rose Thompson, were born there. The home was located in Holmes next to Dave Stockton's family home.

A Miller truck is seen crossing the Van Duzen River on a makeshift log crib bridge bringing in much-needed equipment to the area, as a lot of heavy equipment was lost in the flooding. Thanks to it being a logging community, heavy equipment and the know-how to build bridges were very useful.

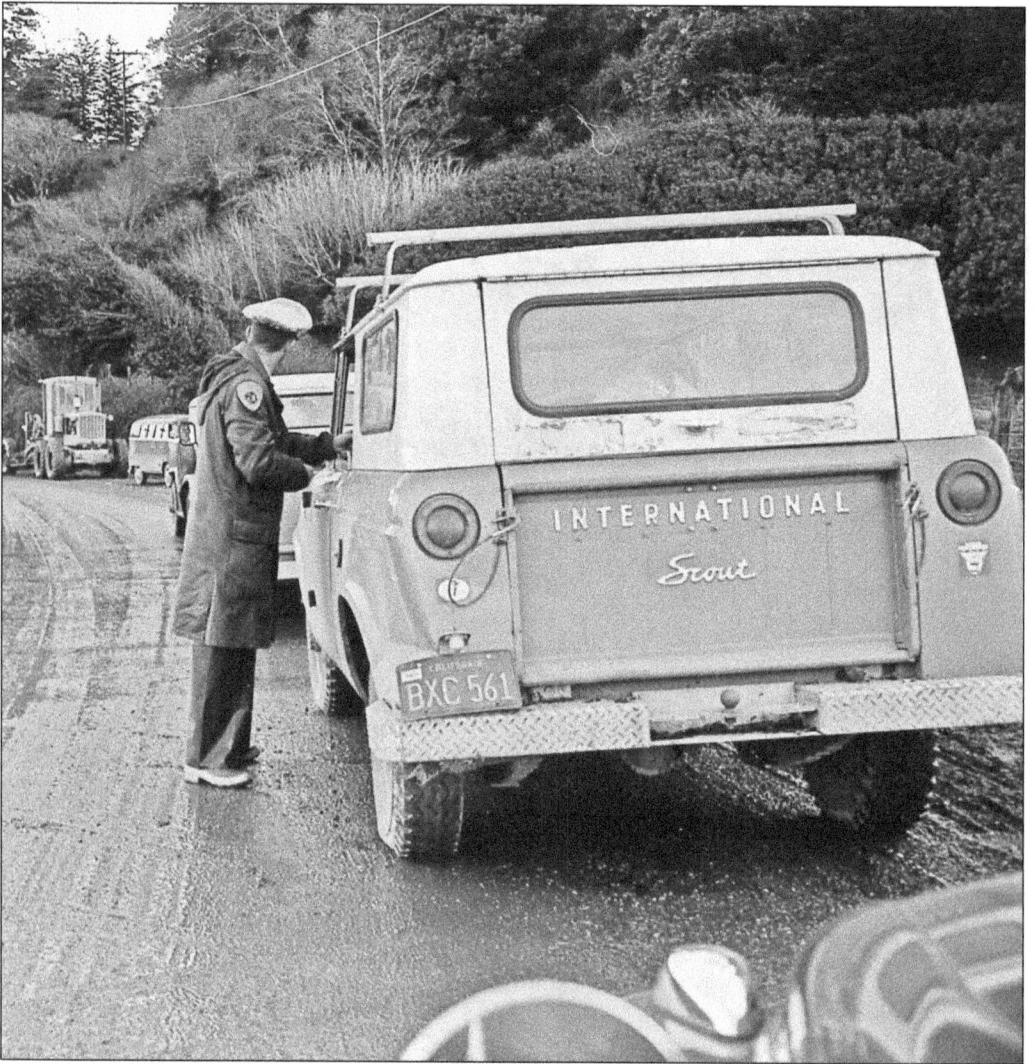

A California Highway Patrol officer is seen talking to a motorist waiting in a convoy line; this was a common scene throughout the area because most of the roads were heavily damaged, necessitating escorts.

This aerial view of the Paul Mudgett Bridge north of Rio Dell shows the mostly completed infrastructure of the bridge; unfortunately, due to the haste of getting the bridge up and running, quick fixes were made that later caused the bridge to fail after another flood and logjam.

Here is another view of the Mudgett Bridge under construction; the main supports were not driven deep enough into bedrock and later washed out. There was such a rush to get bridges back up that shortcuts were taken, which cost millions of dollars to fix later.

This view of the South Rio Dell Scotia Bridge shows just how close a couple of buildings came to falling over the edge. The large structure was saved, but the smaller ones were removed. This was a very important bridge as a large number of people worked at Pacific Lumber Company mill in Scotia and it was their only means of getting to their jobs. So, a simple footbridge was immediately built to get the employees back to work.

Downtown Scotia also became a landing site for helicopters that brought in supplies. This photograph was made out of the window of the main office of the Pacific Lumber Company. Above town, Highway 101 was used as a landing strip for small airplanes.

This book would not of been possible without this man, Rudy Gillard, who was the official flood photographer for the state. Rudy was the business partner of the author, Greg Rumney, during the 1990s, and he donated all of his negatives, which numbered in the several thousands, in order to make a book.

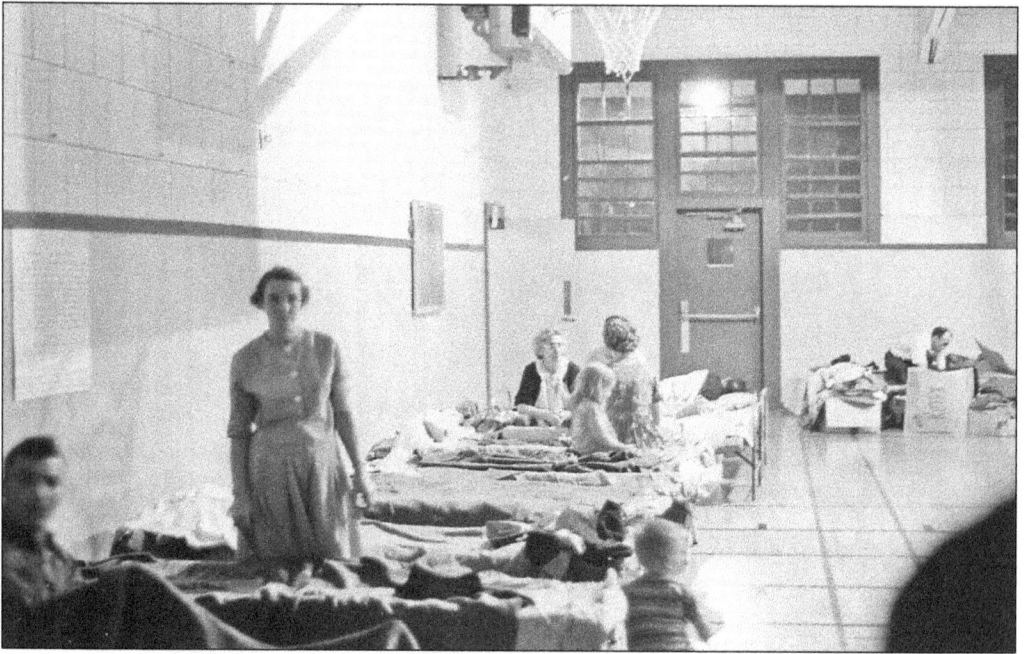

This is a shelter that was set up in Fortuna by the Red Cross to house those who did not have friends or family to stay with. There was such a community outpouring of help that not many people utilized the shelters.

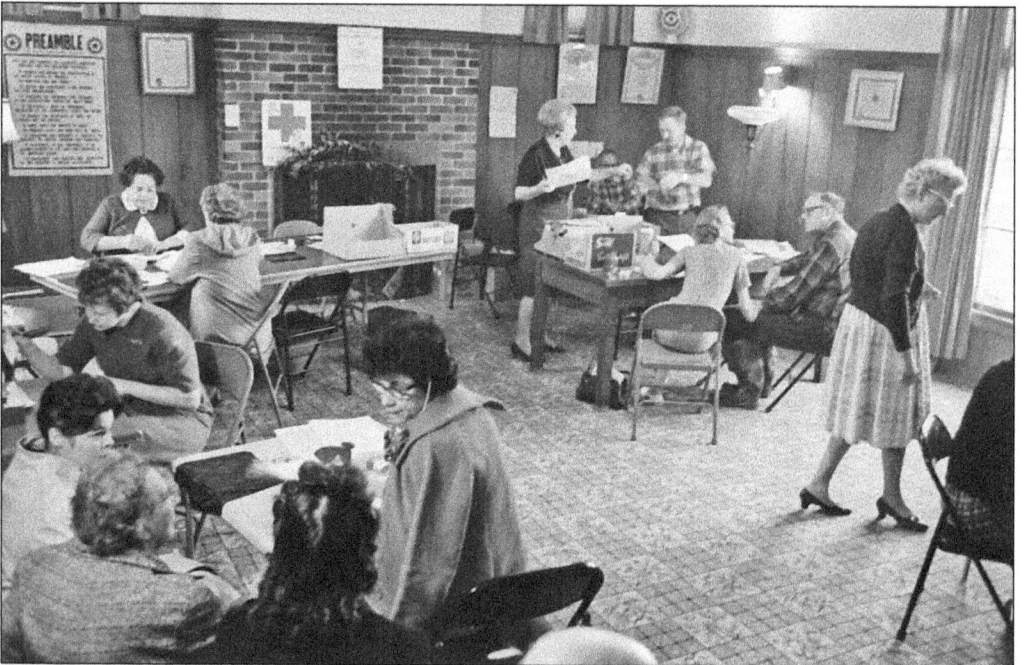

This photograph shows relief workers in the Veteran Building in Fortuna helping those who lost everything; people from all walks of life stepped up to help those in need of food, shelter, and clothing.

This shows just how much debris had to be removed in order to get to the bridge leading into Rio Dell. The span was lost in the flood, and Eel River Sawmill was located to the left and had its log deck spill out onto Highway 101. Lumber mills such as this one opened up at incredible speeds to start producing the needed lumber for the reconstruction effort.

This scene along the Scotia bluffs shows the damage done to the railroad tracks, which connect the west coast to the south. Without the railroad, commerce came to a standstill; the north coast depends on the rail system to ship lumber and other products, so a priority was made to fix it as fast as possible.

A scene from Rohnerville airport shows workers loading much-needed supplies into an airplane. Pilots became heroes to many people as they flew in inclement weather just to deliver supplies to outlying communities cut off from rest of the world. Highway 101 became an airport overnight.

This footbridge was a lifeline for many people who had to go to their jobs in Scotia at the Pacific Lumber Company mill across the river from Rio Dell. Without this bridge, hundreds of people would have been out of work. Pacific Lumber needed all the workers possible to help clean up the mess at the mill.

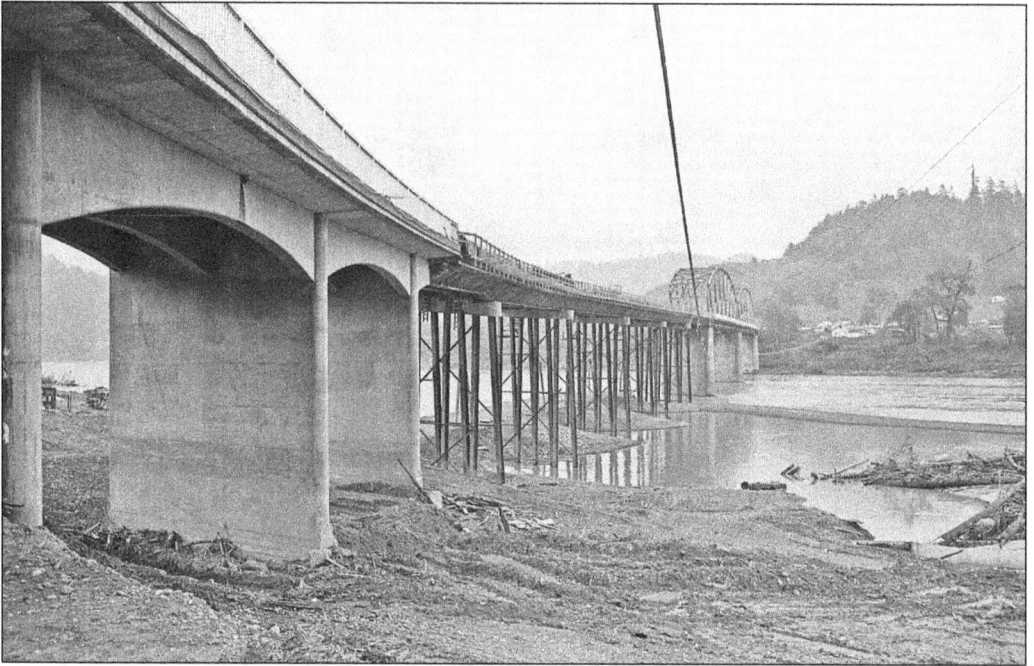

The Paul Mudgett Bridge, linking Rio Dell to the north, is almost complete in this photograph. Without this important link, people would have had to traverse around Blue Slide Road into Ferndale just to get to Eureka. And for quite some time, that route was also closed.

This image shows the point of failure of the dike in Fortuna. Built after the 1955 flood, the dike had a weak section and gave way, allowing floodwaters to inundate the town of Fortuna.

This aerial view shows the completed dike and the area known then as South Twelfth Street, Fortuna. The mill in the foreground with the two teepee burners is the Clay-Brown Mill, which is the present-day site of Eel River Brewing Company. This area was known for its numerous gyppo mills, which dotted this whole area. The mill across the highway is another owned by the Pacific Lumber Company. The area today is dotted with hotels and other businesses.

This photograph shows the dedication of the reopening of Eel River Sawmill, which was located just north of Rio Dell. The mill was all but destroyed by the raging waters of the Eel River.

A local band plays as film crews shoot the reopening of the Paul Mudgett Bridge north of Rio Dell; this was one of the most important bridges in the area.

Guy Maxwell, mayor of Rio Dell, and other important dignitaries cut the ribbon on the new Paul Mudgett Bridge. Hundreds of local people showed up for the event.

Seen here, people walk across the newly opened bridge. Pedestrians are followed by a school bus full of revelers.

Visit us at
arcadiapublishing.com